Just For: Mary Josephene

From:

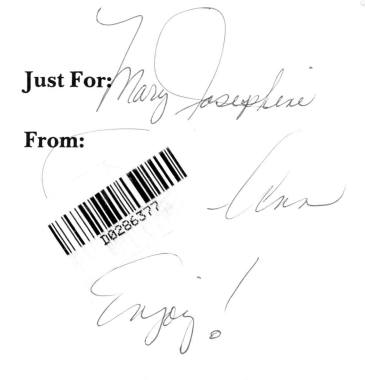

Enjoy!

DOES DINNER IN A BUCKET COUNT?
90 Laughs for the 90's Woman
by Liz Curtis Higgs

Illustrated by Carol L. Cornette

THOMAS NELSON PUBLISHERS
Nashville

Published in Nashville, Tennessee, by Thomas Nelson, Inc., Publishers, and
distributed in Canada by Word Communications, Ltd., Richmond, British
Columbia, and in the United Kingdom by Word (UK), Ltd., Milton Keynes,
England.

Library of Congress Cataloging-in-Publication Data

Higgs, Liz Curtis
   Does dinner in a bucket count? : 90 laughs for the 90's woman
/ by Liz Curtis Higgs : illustrated by Carol L. Cornette.
      p. cm.
   ISBN 0-7852-8283-1 / 0-8407-6995-4 (PPk.)

   1. Women--Humor. 2. Single women--Humor. I. Title.
PN6231.W6H47 1993
818'.5402--dc20   93-2956
                                                                                    CIP

Printed in the United States of America
1 2 3 4 5 6 7 - 98 97 96 95 94 93

This little book is dedicated to every woman who has ever worried about being a bad mother, a terrible cook, an old maid or pregnant for life.

You have a lot of company.

SINGLENESS

As each year goes by, you get a
little less picky.

When I was 21, my list of expectations for Mr. Right would have easily filled a 3-ring notebook.

By 25, the list started getting shorter . . .

... When I hit the Big 3-0, the list was dramatically reduced to a few absolute musts. At 32, it was down to one word: breathing.

Friends who marry have a lot of nerve. They expect you to come to their wedding, be happy for them, *and* bring a gift.

On bad days, the whole world and all that's in it can be described in two words: *Pairs* and *Spares*.

Almost 25,000,000 American men are single. At last count, 43 of them were willing to make a commitment.

Your friendly thesaurus pretty
much sums up "singleness":

Isolated
Alone
Companionless
Deserted
On the loose . . .

... On the other hand,
"singleness" also means:

Exceptional
Unrivaled
Original
Rare
Unique

(You rare, exceptional creature, you!)

Favorite question from married people:

"How is it a nice girl like you isn't married yet?"

(Easy. Nobody asked me.)

Favorite comment from church people:

"God has a man for you."

(He knows my address. What's the holdup?)

When I was single, my married friends were always trying to "fix me up."

Funny. I never felt broken.

Favorite church bulletin notice:

Beginning Again Seminar:
Help for the *Formally* Married

(If you wore a gown and he wore a tux, this one's for you.)

MARRIAGE

The experts say that romance
drops 80% in the first two years
of marriage.

(Really?? That long?)

When Bill (34) and I (32) got married, we had collectively looked for each other for 66 years.

At that point in life, you make a few concessions: he married me big, I married him bald.

I chose a tea-length wedding gown, thinking I'd have lots of opportunities to wear it again. Three problems:

1. It's too tight.
2. It's too white.
3. When I walk in a room, someone starts singing "Here Comes the Bride."

Honeymoon Discovery #1:

Bill was not used to fancy hotels.
He thought the towels were nice
and thick, but much too small.
He was using the bath mat.

According to Spiegel catalog, these are the five most challenging "treasures" a new husband will try to incorporate into his bride's decorating scheme . . .

...Deer horns   Weights
Stuffed fish   Moose heads
Potbellied stoves

(And you thought what YOU ended up with was awful!)

True story from a woman in Milwaukee:

When the butcher shop in her husband's hometown finally closed their doors, they auctioned off all the fixtures, and hubby ended up with a six foot neon chicken...

. . ."Where is it now?" I asked her.

"In our dining room," she said. "And when we have chicken, we turn it on."

You've heard couples say,
"Someday we'll laugh about this."
Why wait?

Once I ran out of deodorant and had to use Bill's. I walked around all day smelling like pine logs on a wood-burning stove.

Yes, you're married, but do you like him?

First Year: Iffy.
Second Year: No.
Third Year: Sometimes.
Fourth Year: Fairly often.
Fifth Year: A keeper.

PREGNANCY

Pregnancy so consumes you that you wonder what in the world you used to think about.

Being pregnant means adjusting to complete strangers patting your tummy and telling you something even your doctor isn't certain of: "Now, *that's* a girl!"

Ultrasound:

A womb with a view

Co-workers and friends ask the same three questions, over and over:

1. "When are you due?"
2. "Have you picked out your names yet?"
3. "What do you want, a boy or girl?"

... I finally gave up and pinned a sign to my maternity jumper:

I love meeting very thin pregnant women and saying, "You know, I used to be about your size until I started having children."

(It isn't true, of course, but it really shakes them up!)

Ask a first-time mother what her due date is and she'll tell you the exact day. A second-timer will tell you the month. The veteran just says, "Spring."

After two or three baby showers, an expectant mom has amassed several quarts of baby oil. Who in their right mind would squirt oil on a wet, slippery baby?

Bill thought all that baby oil might keep the little one from squeaking.

(Groan here.)

Mothers-to-be suddenly worry about everything, even stray electronic fields and hidden x-rays. I distinctly remember starting my microwave oven with a pencil.

An expectant woman is often called "glowing" and "radiant." It's really sweat.

By the ninth month, the little
mother is in full-tilt waddle, with
swollen ankles, an itchy tummy
and an outie belly button.
Walking up steps, she discovers
the bottom of her stomach is
touching the tops of her thighs . . .

... No longer able to cross her legs, and reduced to sleeping upright in an overstuffed chair, a pregnant woman's greatest fear is that she'll sneeze unexpectedly and wet her pants.

So much for radiance.

CHILDBIRTH

It is not your imagination: labor does last forever. Why do you think we celebrate Labor Day in September and Mother's Day in May?

I was determined to make my Lamaze instructor proud of me by going through labor without drugs. The first twelve hours, we breathed. The next six, we tried laughing away the pain.

Finally, my anesthesiologist showed up with a big button that read: "Just Say YES!"

Our son Matthew was the Blue Ribbon winner at the Kentucky State Fair for "Biggest Baby of 1987," tipping the scales at 11 pounds, 12 1/2 ounces.

(Why have a baby when you can have a toddler?)

Women often ask if I delivered
my enormous children
"naturally." "Oh yes!" I tell them.
"I laid a large egg and sat on it
for nine months."

I still can't believe that two people with no prior experience can take home a baby . . .

... After all, when we bought our new car, we had to read the warranty in the presence of our salesman, watch a video, and sign a waiver.

But a newborn? Not even so much as a postcard in the mail asking, "Are you happy with your new purchase?"

MOTHERHOOD

All mothers need eyes in the back of their head, and ears in the back of their house.

Motherhood is not only the oldest profession, it's the hardest: the hours are atrocious, the pay is the pits, and the benefits are . . . well, the little angels have you there.

Favorite nursing mother question: "If I lie out in the sun, will my milk sour?"

In today's economy, it costs $150,000 to get a child from birth to 18. More, if you use brand name diapers.

Inside the label on Gerber baby food is the following warning: "DO NOT FEED FROM THE JAR."

For mothers who unwittingly spooned their baby's applesauce directly from jar to mouth, a support group is being formed.

Favorite Pediatric Advice:

"To relieve a persistent rash,
leave the diaper off for a few
hours."

Now on grocery shelves:
A pacifier that "glows in the
dark for easier locating."

What if it's under the couch?
I want one that beeps when you
clap your hands.

Parental Rule: Do not be enticed into buying 50 wallet-size photos of your child if you know only eleven people.

HOUSEWORK

I used to think that no one could clean my house as well as I could. Then I took a good look around and said, "Who am I kidding?"

A nationwide survey of husbands in two-career marriages revealed:

30% wash dishes (1% wipe counters)

28% shop for groceries (send with detailed list)

25% can cook (will use at least eight pots and pans per meal)

22% help clean house, and

18% do laundry (the other 82% take it home to their mothers)

Madison Avenue fables:

Needs no ironing
Shatterproof bottle
Some assembly required
Covers in one coat
Shrink-resistant

I know it's time to mop
the kitchen floor when
walking across it
hurts my feet.

Dust Bunnies make great pets.
You don't have to feed them or
take them for walks, and they
don't leave puddles on the rug.
Usually, they hide under a
chair waiting for company to
arrive so they can
roll out, wrapped
around a sock.

Bill once said, "I'd rather come home to a happy wife than a clean house."

He got his wish.

COOKING

Who says I'm not a gourmet
cook? I've been serving
blackened food for years.

Good news: I'm married to a man who will eat anything.

Bill: "Hey, this is delicious! Can we have it again?"

Liz: "No. I don't know what it is."

Some women have little signs that say, "Kathy's Kitchen" or "Kiss the Cook." Mine says "UFO* Sighting."

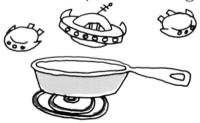

Unidentified Frying Objects

I only buy cookbooks for the pictures.

My favorite casserole recipe:

Combine everything
from the left
side of the fridge.
Put potato chips
on top. Bake.

Mother's rule of food preparation:

Bake it at 350 degrees until it
stops moving.

In nearly forty years of living, a few of which have included cooking, I've never used more than four potatoes in a 5-lb. sack. Every few months, I carry another red mesh bag to the garbage can, arms outstretched, trying not to accidentally touch the waving tentacles.

Please raise your hand
if you've ever found
critters in your flour.

Thank you.

Bill is really a much better cook than I am, but he requires watching. He once tried to use an egg slicer to cut mushrooms (too rubbery).

I've also learned to keep our children's clothing safely away from kitchen counters, after mild-mannered Bill got so carried away with a meat cleaver he whacked off part of the sleeve of Lillian's discarded yellow coat. (He thought it was a chicken breast.)

More than 70% of American homes now have microwave ovens. I suspect 69% of us only use REHEAT.

BACK TO SCHOOL

The harsh truth about going to college as an adult: the desks don't fit.

A whole roomful of 17-year olds
will ask, "How old *are* you?"

The sweater you're wearing is
older than they are.

Your husband will tell people he is living with a college student.

You alone will do the reading and ace the tests. You will blow the grading curve, and your classmates will hate it. Especially when you graduate *summa cum laude.* Go for it.

GUILT

It's tough to use a laptop computer when you no longer have a lap.

My audiences often ask me if I miss my children when I'm on the road speaking.

Sure.

But it *is* nice to look out at a whole roomful of people who dressed themselves.

For moms who travel, airport card shops now feature colorful greeting cards to mail to your kids back home. They have warm thoughts inside like, "Can't wait to hug you again," or "Mama misses you s-o-o-o-o much."

I vote for more realism: "Have you cleaned your room yet?"

If you ask women what they want more of in their lives, they never shout out, "Sex!" or "Money!" Their response is always the same: "Time!"

(I know, I know: If you had more TIME, you also might have more of the other two.)

What single women hear:

"Why don't you get out more? You'll never meet someone sitting at home."

What married women hear:

"So when are you going to start a family?"

What mothers at home hear:

"What do you DO all day?"

What working mothers hear:

"But who cares for your children while you work?"

GUILT TABLE:
(on a scale of 1 to 10)

Falling asleep during
the 6:00 PM news 2

Sending store-bought
cookies to school 5

Forgetting to pick up
child (1st time) 9

Forgetting to pick up
child (2nd time) 342

A working mother in Lansing wrote, "There just isn't enough of ME to go around."

(Some of us don't have this problem.)

The hardest word in the English language can be found right in the middle of the alphabet:

My goal for the new year:

"Better done than perfect."

ENCOURAGEMENT

A good compliment is better than a massage.

Wisdom from a friend:

There are no such things as bad days . . . only bad moments in good days.

Life is like a VCR.

If you're constantly moving in FAST FORWARD, your days will be a blur. If you're always reaching for REWIND, you'll miss some nice surprises.

Instead, enjoy life in the PLAY mode, content with each frame that passes before your eyes.

So . . . *does* dinner in a bucket , bag,
or box *count*?

Of course!

It's not what's in the bucket
that matters, it's the woman
who's holding it: *you!*

THE END

About the illustrator . . .

Carol L. Cornette is an
independent illustrator,
graphic designer and writer
in Louisville, Kentucky.

When she learned how to
spell it in late 1986, she decided
to become an *entrepreneur*.

Carol L. Cornette
502-897-6787

About the Author . . .

Liz Curtis Higgs is a professional speaker, humorist, author, businesswoman, singer, mother and wife -- on some days, all at the same time. (She was recently selected for *Who's <u>That</u> of American Women!*)

For more information about her books, tapes and presentations, contact:

Liz Curtis Higgs
AN ENCOURAGER.

P.O. Box 43577
Louisville, Kentucky 40253-0577